21 THINGS to do with A MUD PIE

JANE WILSHER & TEO GEORGIEV

IVY KIDS

21 Things to Do With a Mud Pie

Here are 21 squelchy, soil-loving things to do with a mud pie...

I'm testing my mud. That's number 3.

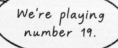

We're playing number 19.

I'm doing number 18, painting with mud.

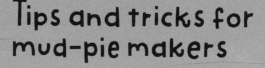

Tips and tricks for mud-pie makers

When you are on a muddy nature adventure, follow the mud-pie lover's code.

This book is packed with outside muddy fun. There are a few growing activities that you can do inside, too.

When you play outside in the mud, always take your adult with you. Ask them to help with the activities.

Find a safe place for your muddy play with soil that you're allowed to dig up. You'll also need water nearby.

Don't touch soil that has been near chemicals, including on a farm.

Make sure no one eats your mud pies!

When you go home, take everything with you that doesn't belong outside.

When you've finished playing with your mud pie, wash your hands in warm soapy water for at least 30 seconds. Rub soap between your fingers, then rinse with water. Dry your hands on a clean towel.

Make mud-pie muffins, that's number 14.

Shout HOORAY for mud pies!

Mud, soil, dirt, earth: it's all the same and it all helps to make a really good mud pie. Soil does so much for us, so let's go outside and shout hip, hip, hooray for mud pies!

Farmers plant fruit, vegetables, rice, and beans in the soil for us to eat.

All kinds of animals live in the soil. Rabbits make their home in a maze of underground tunnels.

When it rains, plants help to stop the soil from washing away.

Beneath my feet, there are layers of soil and rock. I'm standing on the topsoil.

A seed grows into a plant in the soil. When the plant dies, its remains help to make the soil rich, ready for a new plant to grow.

Worms, beetles, and ants wriggle, burrow, and march, making pockets of air that help new plants to grow.

1 Choose the mud for your pie

First, choose a safe muddy place outside where you can dig and play. Remember, don't make your mud pies inside.

Where will you make your pies?

- Look out for mud kitchens and mud workshops at school or in a local park or woodland.

- Or make your own mud-play area outside. Ask your adult to make sure it's safe and that you're allowed to play with the mud.

- You will need a faucet, and a bottle or watering can to fill with water.

- You can gather old pots, pans, and flower pots. Sticks make good spoons, too.

I'm wearing an apron to stop the mud from getting everywhere!

Playing in mud makes me feel happy.

I'm fetching the watering can.

When I finish, I'll wash my hands.

These are old pots, pans, and containers.

Now the fun begins!

It's time to get muddy and grubby and make some mud pies. And along the way, don't be surprised if you learn all kinds of things about soil and why it's so useful. Always look out for the muddy clues in nature.

2 Make a mud pie

Go on, put your fingers into your pie and feel all the squelchy mud.

Mix up a mud pie

You will need

Soil and water, an old bowl, old pots and containers for molds, a stick or old spoon for stirring, and some leaves.

Here's how!

Mix the soil and water in the bowl to make a thick gloop. Scoop it into an old pot, then dollop it onto a leaf. Make more pies. Do it your way. Have fun!

3 Ask your mud pie questions

Yes, really, you can talk to your mud pie! When you carry out tests on the soil, your pie will tell you about the soil where you live. First, ask what the mud feels like.

Is it gritty? Yes! It's **sandy soil.**

If you can roll it into a shiny ball, it's **clay.**

Is it gritty and sticky? Then it's **loam,** which is a mixture of sand and clay.

What's soil made from?

- Minerals, which are parts of old rock
- The remains of dead plants and animals
- Small holes, or pockets, of air and water

Test your mud pie

Make a jar test to find out the type of soil in your mud pie.

You will need

One of your mud pies, a glass jar with a lid, and water.

Here's how!

1 Fill the jar less than halfway with your mud pie or similar soil.

2 Add water almost to the top. Put on the lid and shake hard. Don't move the jar for a few hours.

3 There should now be layers of mud and water in the jar.

4 What kind of soil makes the biggest layer: sand, silt, or clay? That's the type of soil in your area.

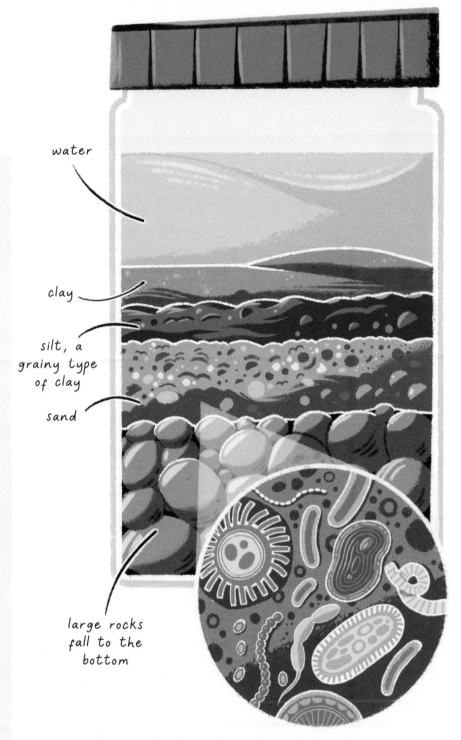

water

clay

silt, a grainy type of clay

sand

large rocks fall to the bottom

Different places have different kinds of soil. This test result shows the soil in the jar is sandy.

What's mud like up close?

In one teaspoon of soil, there are over one billion microbes, which are tiny living things too small to see. Microbes pack the soil with goodness.

4 Meet your mud pie's animal friends

Animals tiny and tall dig dark, underground homes, where they eat, sleep, and have babies. When your mud pie was soil in the ground, it was home to many different animals.

Look out for...

...signs of animals living underground.

Search for cracks that insects might crawl through to the soil below.

Mounds of earth might be the way in or out of a home for a bigger animal, such as a mole, a rabbit, or a fox.

A rabbit digs with its front paws, kicking the soil behind.

Earthworms wriggle up to the surface to gather leaves to eat.

A big group of rabbits lives together in an underground home, called a warren.

Why do animals live underground?

It can be safer under the soil, out of the reach of hungry enemies. In the fall, some animals dig underground homes where they hibernate, or sleep all winter.

There is a maze of tunnels with side rooms, where the rabbits live and have babies.

If a predator tries to attack through one entrance, the rabbits can make a getaway through another.

A bug points its bottom upward, then burrows head first into the earth.

Foxes live in holes called dens. You might find signs of a den by a wall or under a shed.

Wood mice keep nuts and seeds safe in an underground nest, just like a food cupboard.

A mole digs a tunnel with paws that scoop and look like shovels.

Watch wild animals safely from a distance. **Never** approach or touch these animals.

9

5 Make a wormery

Wriggling worms keep the soil full of air holes.
Make a wormery and watch worms at work.

Build a wormery

You will need

A large, clean glass jar or see-through container, damp soil, sand, old leaves, a rubber band, a piece of fabric to fit over the top of the jar, scissors, black paper, and a few wriggling worms.

Look out for...

. . . earthworms after it's been raining or early in the morning.

Look for worms under rocks, stones, and piles of leaves.

Pick worms that have come above the ground. Don't pull them out of the soil.

As you gather the worms, be gentle with them and keep them safe.

Here's how

1 Sprinkle a thin layer of sand in the jar, then add a thick layer of soil. Make more layers in this way to fill up the jar.

2 Put a layer of old leaves on top of the soil.

3 Now it's time to add your worms.

Why are worms good for the soil?

Worms burrow and make tunnels, which help plants to grow. Worms also make good things for the soil, called nutrients. They take leaves underground to eat, then poop the nutrients from the leaves into the soil.

4 Snip small air holes in the fabric. Cover the opening with the fabric and stretch the rubber band over the top.

5 Wrap the black paper around the jar. Now wash your hands.

6 Keep your wormery in a cool, dark place for a day or two.

Look at how your worms wriggle up and down the wormery, gathering leaves.

Worms like damp but not very wet soil, so water your wormery with trickles of water.

If the leaves run out, give the worms some more.

Whenever you want to study the worms, take off the black paper.

Notice the tunnels of air.

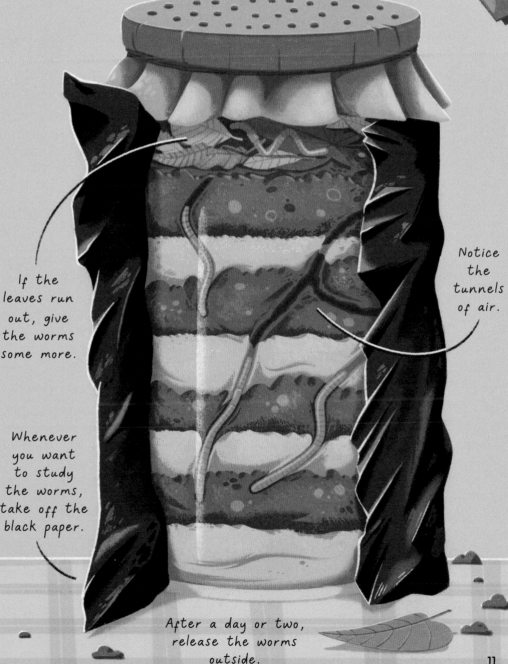

After a day or two, release the worms outside.

6 Build an ant-arium

Have you ever watched a line of ants walking along? They might have been looking for food to take back to their nest in the soil.

Make an ants' home

You will need

A large clean jar with a lid, a smaller clean jar and lid which fits inside the bigger jar, sand, soil, a small piece of sponge, a small chunk of apple, an elastic band, black paper, and a piece of gauze to fit over the large jar.

Ask an adult to help make holes in the lid of the large jar.

Here's how!

1 Screw the lid on the small jar and place it upside down inside the large jar, so there's space between the two jars.

2 Mix about one teaspoon of soil with a handful of sand. Spoon the mixture between the jars and over the top of the smaller jar.

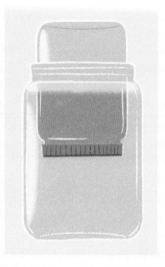

3 Wet the sponge and place it on top of the sand and soil.

4 Put a chunk of apple on top of the sponge.

5 Ask your adult to poke air holes into the lid of the large jar.

6 Now find some ants to live in your ant-arium. Look under a rock or near leaves. Use a leaf to brush the ants gently into the jar.

7 To stop the ants from escaping, place the gauze on top of the jar. Keep it in place with a rubber band.

8 Screw on the lid with air holes. Then wrap black paper around the jar and tape it in place. Now wash your hands.

It's important to **look after your ants** and keep them **safe**, because they are **living creatures.**

The ants need air, water, and fresh food to eat.

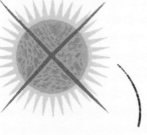

Never leave your ant-arium out in the sunshine.

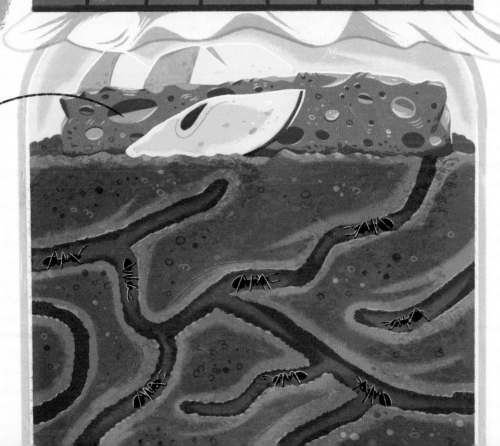

Unwrap the jar to watch the ants take fruit down into their tunnels.

After a few days, release the ants outside.

Make prints in your mud pie

Next time you walk in wet mud, look behind you to see your muddy footprints. When the sun dries the mud hard, your footprints will still be there.

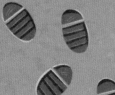

What happens to the mud in the rain and the sun?

In the rain, a muddy path might be full of puddles and difficult to pass. But in hot weather, when the sun bakes the mud hard, there might be deep cracks.

Look out for...

...signs of who's been where in the mud. Can you find the following, either in wet, sticky mud or mud that's baked hard?

Make prints in mud

You will need

Some clay, or mud that feels like soft modeling clay, an old rolling pin, and things from nature, such as shells or leaves, or small toys with wheels.

Here's how!

1 Roll out the mud or clay so it's flat.

2 The easiest print to make is with your hands. Press your palm and fingers into the mud.

3 Now try making different prints and tracks in the mud with all kinds of shells, leaves, and toys.

4 Leave the prints to dry.

birds' claw prints

bicycle tracks

dogs' paw prints

shoe prints

Make a fossil

You will need

An adult to help you, a mixing bowl, a wooden spoon, small toys or shells, goggles, and a small hammer.

- 2 tablespoons flour
- 2 tablespoons old coffee grounds
- 1 tablespoon salt
- 5 tablespoons of soil
- About 1 ½ tablespoons of water

What's a fossil?

It's the shape of an animal or a plant that has been pressed into rock. A fossil is made when mud squeezes into the shape left by a dead plant or animal. Over thousands of years, the rock above presses the mud in the shape until it becomes hard.

Here's how!

1 Mix the flour, coffee, salt, and soil in the bowl. Add the water slowly until you have a stiff sandy mixture.

2 Take a handful of the mixture in your hand. Then place a small toy or shell on top. Add more mixture so it's covered. It should look like a smooth rock.

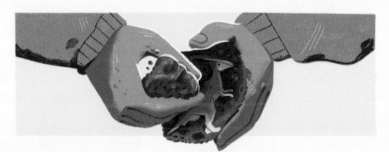

3 Make lots of rocks with fossils inside.

4 Put your rocks in the sunshine or leave them inside on a windowsill until completely dry.

5 Put on your goggles, then smash open the rocks and find your pretend fossils inside.

8

You can do this activity **inside**.

Plant a seed in the soil

It's mud magic! Plant a seed in the soil from your mud pie. The roots will grow under the ground and its stem will grow above the ground.

Grow a plant in a pot

You will need

A flower pot with holes in the bottom, a plant saucer, soil or potting compost, water, and a bean seed or another type of seed that is easy to grow.

Here's how!

1 Fill the plant pot with soil almost to the top.

2 Push your finger into the soil to make a little hole.

3 Drop the seed into the hole then cover it up with the soil.

4 Put the pot on the saucer. Water the soil, but not too much.

5 Keep the pot on a sunny windowsill and water it when the soil looks dry. How long does it take for green shoots to appear?

9 Race sunflowers

In the spring, plant sunflowers outside. Which will grow tallest?

Plant sunflowers

You will need

A pack of sunflower seeds, a small gardening trowel and fork, bamboo canes, garden string, a bottle or watering can full of water, and a tape measure.

Here's how!

1 Pull up any weeds from the ground. Dig the top of the soil so it feels loose and crumbly. Water the soil, too.

2 Use your finger to make a little hole. Drop one seed into the hole and cover it with soil.

Water your sunflowers and watch them grow.

Is your sunflower taller than you? Measure to find out.

8 inches

3 Measure about 8 inches along and plant another seed. Plant a few more seeds in a row. Water the soil with a watering can.

4 To protect your seedlings from hungry slugs and snails, you can place a cut plastic bottle over each of the young plants with green shoots.

5 As your sunflower begins to grow, prop it up with a cane and tie it in place with string.

Did you guess which sunflower would grow the tallest?

10 Plant a butterfly garden

Nature is full of round-and-round stories about the lives of plants and animals. These stories are called lifecycles. They show how nature is a circle of life.

This is the round-and-round story of **butterflies**, **flowers**, and the **soil**.

1 One day, a butterfly lands on a flower . . .

2 The butterfly unfurls its long tongue and drinks a sweet juice, called nectar.

3 Inside the flower, there's a powder that helps new plants to grow. It's called pollen.

4 Pollen from the plant's stamen sticks to the butterfly.

5 When the butterfly visits another flower, the pollen finds its way to the plant's stigma and a new seed starts to grow.

6 Inside the plant, a seed forms. The seed ends up in the soil.

7 Soon, a new plant grows tall and flowery.

stigma

pollen

stamen

stigma

pollen

Butterflies are called pollinators because they carry pollen from plant to plant.

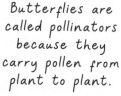

Which plants attract butterflies?

Butterflies visit brightly colored, sweet-smelling flowers, such as daisies, lilac, and parsley. Ask an adult which plants grow well in your area and attract butterflies.

Plant a butterfly garden in the spring

You will need

A small gardening trowel and fork, a bottle or watering can full of water, and seeds or seedlings, which are little plants.

When the soil becomes dry, water your butterfly garden.

Watch your plants grow and butterflies come to drink nectar.

To give butterflies a place to drink, fill an old saucer with wet sand.

Here's how!

1 Look for a sunny spot near bushes and rocks, where the butterflies might sun themselves.

2 First, prepare the soil by digging and making sure the soil is damp.

3 To plant seeds, follow the instructions on the packet. Plant each seed just below the surface. Then water the soil.

4 To plant a seedling, dig a hole for each seedling, then fill the hole with soil. Water the soil.

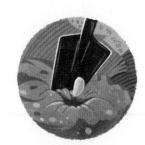

Look out for...

... small, yellow chunks of powdery pollen in the middle of a flower.

Bees buzzing! Bees are also pollinators and help new flowers to grow.

11 Grow lunch in the mud

Now it's time to plant and grow your own food to eat

The beans are ready when they are green and as long as a finger

Grow a bean wigwam

Plant your beans in the spring or summer.

You will need

A small gardening trowel and fork, a bottle or watering can full of water, a packet of climbing bean seeds, six bamboo canes, and garden string.

Here's how!

1 Choose a sunny spot. Pull out any weeds from the soil. Then dig the soil so it's crumbly. You might need to water the soil, too.

2 Stick the six canes into the soil about 12 inches apart. Imagine your patch of soil is a clock face and place the canes at 12, 2, 4, 6, 8, and 10.

3 Ask your adult to tie the canes together at the top with string to make a wigwam shape.

4 Help your adult to tie a knot at the bottom of one cane. Take the string to the next cane and tie another knot. Crisscross the string all the way up.

5 At the bottom of each cane, dig a small hole. Drop one seed into each hole. Cover the holes with soil. Then water the soil.

6 Over the next few weeks, water the soil if it becomes dry.

7 Soon shoots and curly tails will grow. Wind them around the string so they grow up the wigwam. When the beans are ready, ask your adult how to pod and cook them.

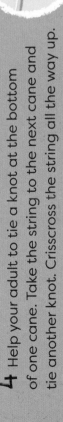

Try planting different foods. Look at the seed packet to find out when and how to plant the seeds. Or plant a small plant, called a seedling.

What food grows in the soil?

Fruit and vegetables grow in orchards and on farms. Apples and oranges grow on trees. Wheat and rice grow in fields. A vegetable patch might be full of tomatoes, strawberries, and beans.

A tomato plant grows tall. It needs to lean on a stick.

A strawberry plant grows near the ground. It loves sunshine.

Look out for...

...signs that the fruit and vegetables you eat grew on plants in the ground.

The marks on potatoes are left by old roots.

The pips inside oranges and apples are seeds.

The pointy end of a carrot is the bottom of the root.

Shake arugula seeds on the soil and water them. Watch them grow.

12 Watch things rot in mud

Rotten stuff is good, not bad! Your mud pie can turn what we think of as garbage into goodness for the soil.

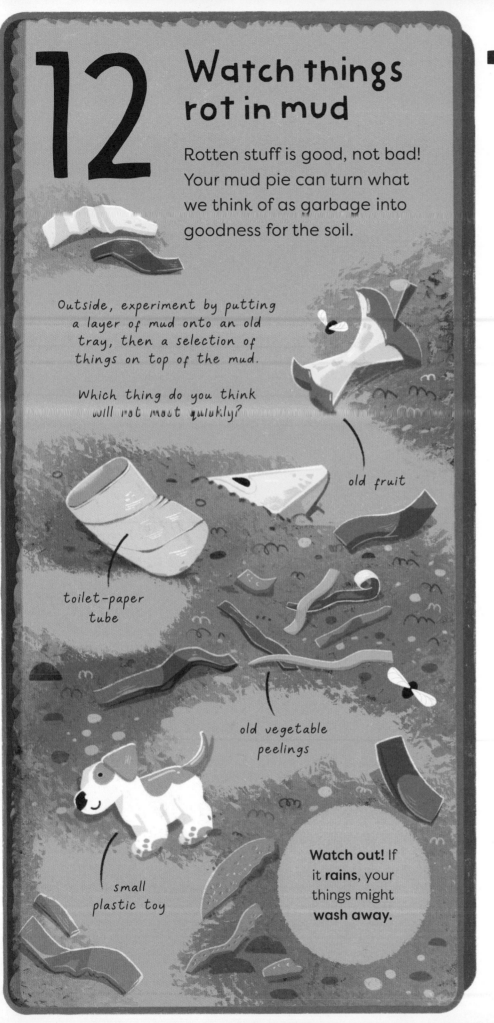

Outside, experiment by putting a layer of mud onto an old tray, then a selection of things on top of the mud.

Which thing do you think will rot most quickly?

old fruit

toilet-paper tube

old vegetable peelings

small plastic toy

Watch out! If it **rains**, your things might **wash away.**

13

Make a compost bottle

Composting is great for the soil. Old food scraps rot to become compost, which helps to make the soil rich and full of goodness.

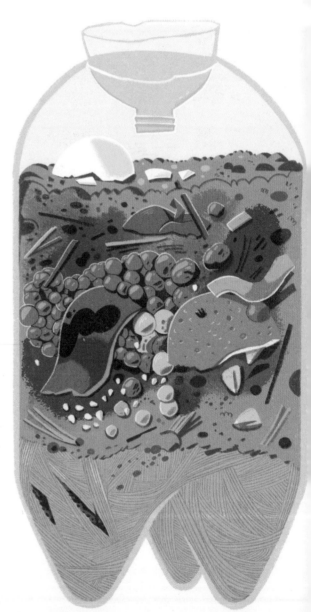

You will need

A clean, clear 2-liter plastic bottle, a thumb tack, soil, water, and old food scraps.

Here's how!

1 Ask your adult to cut off the top of the bottle and pierce the bottom with the thumb tack to make lots of holes.

2 Shake in a layer of soil. Now add all kinds of food scraps. Then place the top of the bottle upside down in the neck.

Look out for...

...flies buzzing near compost. Flies eat rotting food, then poop out good things that make the compost rich. New flies also hatch on the compost.

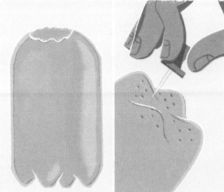

In a garden, a **compost bin or pile** works in the same way as your compost bottle, just on a bigger scale.

vegetable peelings

eggshells

fruit peel

torn paper

Don't add meat, cat litter, or anything plastic.

3 Dribble in some water.

4 Place your bottle in a warm, covered place outside.

5 Over the coming days and weeks, watch the rotting stuff become rich compost. Feed this compost to your plants.

23

14 Make a mud-pie kitchen

Set up a mud-pie kitchen outside and bake pretend muddy dishes in the sunshine. What's on the menu? Mud soup, mud doughnuts, mud muffins. . . you decide!

Set up your mud kitchen

You will need

A safe place outside with plenty of soil, a faucet and a bottle or watering can to fill with water, an old bowl, and old pots and trays to shape your pies.

Find a good spot for your kitchen. You can work on a table or on the ground. You need space to make your pies, plus a place to leave them to dry.

Seed pods and nutshells become pots and containers.

Mud soup

In a bowl, add enough water to the soil to make a sloppy soup mixture. What sprinkles will you add?

Stir the gloopy mud with a twig.

Smalll pebbles?

Crunchy sand?

Snapped twigs?

Mud muffins

In a bowl, add water to your soil to make a thick squidgy mixture.

Dollop the mixture into the holes in an old muffin tray.

Don't forget to decorate. What toppings will you add?

Use petals, leaves, and twigs on the ground. **Never** pick anything from living plants.

muffins

Press petals, leaves,
and seeds into
the mud to make
decorations.

Mud doughnuts

Add enough water to the soil to make a
stiff mixture you can hold in your hands.

Shape a small amount in one hand to
make a doughnut shape.

Try making a ring doughnut by pushing
your thumb through the middle.

cake

doughnuts

Big leaves make plates
and serving platters.

Muddy layer cake

Make a big mud pie for one of your pretend layer cakes.

What kind of filling will you make? Bark chippings, grass
cuttings, gravel? Put the filling on top of the mud pie.

Now make another mud pie the same size.
Carefully place it on top of the other mud pie and filling.

Cover your pretend layer cake with all kinds of
sprinkles and decorations.

When you've
finished playing
with mud,
**always wash
your hands.**

15 Make mud-pie bricks

What will you build with your mud bricks?
A tower or a wall or something else?

You will need

Soil, water, grass cuttings, sand, and an old ice-cube tray or small brick-shape containers.

Here's how!

1 Make a thick mixture of mud and water. Try adding grass cuttings or sand to make the mixture stiffer.

2 Squish the mud into an old ice-cube tray. Or use an old container as a mold to make lots of the same shape of brick.

3 Leave the bricks to dry in the sunshine. This can take many days. Then loosen the bricks out of the molds.

16 Design a mud building

Imagine being a mud-pie architect. You can design and build whatever you like. What will it be?

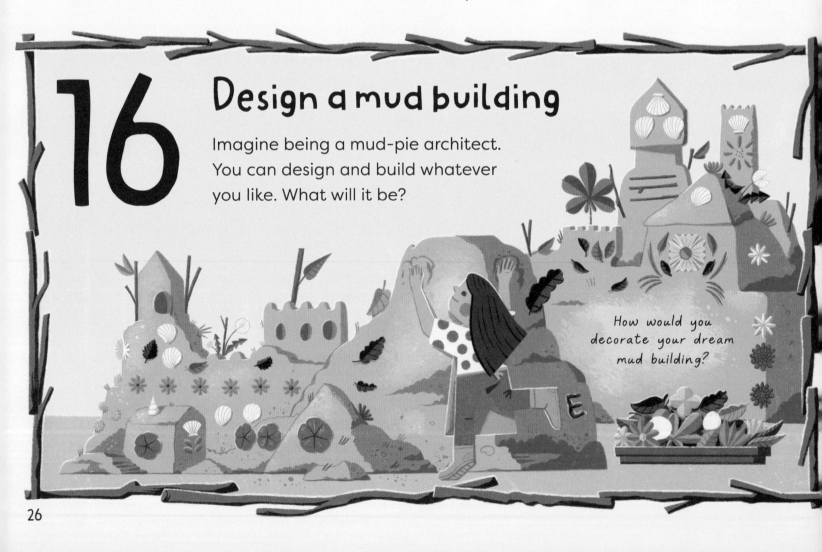

How would you decorate your dream mud building?

17 Make a muddy river

Rivers crisscross the land and push their way through the soil. Smaller rivers shoot off the bigger rivers and look like long spindly fingers.

You will need

A muddy area outside, a shovel, stones, sticks, and a bottle or watering can. You can also do this activity in an old plastic tub.

Here's how!

Scoop out a path for your river. Now pour in water from the watering can, a little at a time. Experiment to see what happens next.

What happens when you put stones at the bottom and up the sides of the riverbed?

What happens when you add sticks, as if they are trees?

What happens when you make small rivers shoot off the big river?

What happens when you build a bridge?

Does your river flow or flood? When the mud flows away with the water, it's called **erosion**.

18 Paint with mud

Become a mud artist! Paint with runny mud and make brushes from leaves and twigs.

Add more or less mud to make your mud paint darker or lighter.

You will need

Soil, water, a bowl for mixing, twigs, leaves, rubber bands, dish soap, and a large sheet of paper.

Here's how!

1 First make the brushes. Choose a twig about 12 inches long.

2 Find some big leaves. Tie them to the end of the twig with a rubber band. Make a few more brushes with different-shaped leaves.

3 To make the paint, in a bowl, slowly add water to mud until it's runny. Add a squirt of dish soap to help it spread. Stir with a twig.

4 Dip your leaf brushes in the muddy paint and paint a wonderful muddy picture.

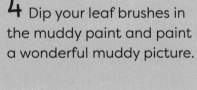

Try this!

Paint with thick mud, then scratch on patterns with a twig.

19 Play stuck in the mud

It's time to play chase and pretend that your feet are firmly stuck in the mud!

Here's how!

This is a game to play outside with four or more friends.

1 Choose one friend to be "it." This friend runs around and tries to catch and tag all the other players.

it

This player is safe and can't be tagged.

3 The only way you can be set free is for a player who hasn't been tagged to crawl through your legs.

2 When you are tagged, you are "stuck in the mud." Stand with your legs apart as if your feet are planted firmly in the ground. Put your arms up, too.

Anyone tagged is "stuck in the mud."

The game **ends** when everyone has been **tagged** and is **stuck** in the **mud.**

20 Thank your mud pie

It's time to thank the soil for all its superpowers, from being the ground beneath our feet to the place where seeds grow into the food we eat.

Gardening gives me a **happy vibe.**

When it rains, mighty trees and smaller plants help keep the soil in place.

What have you eaten today that came from a plant?

When there is too much of a gas called carbon, the Earth heats up. Soil helps to keep the world at just the right temperature by absorbing, or taking in, carbon.

I'm planting next year's tomatoes.

In the beginning, a seed grows in the soil. Then a plant grows.

When the plant dies, it makes the soil rich for a new seed to grow.

Animals tiny and tall, wrigglers and jumpers live in the soil.

21 Look after the mud in your pie

Now that you know why soil is so special, why not look after the soil by spending more time outside planting flowers, fruit, and vegetables?

To keep our planet healthy, we need to look after the soil. Rich soil can be home to all kinds of living things, including billions of microbes, and many species of plants and animals. This is called biodiversity.

Remember, compost rules! Recycle old food to help make nature go round and round.

The world needs more plants, so pick up a shovel and start planting. You could grow plants that bees and butterflies love to visit.

☑ Try to plant flowers that help the planet. Ask locally which plants in your area help make nitrogen in the soil.

☑ All kinds of animals love messy gardens, so please don't tidy up too much.

21 Things to Do with a Mud Pie © 2024 Quarto Publishing plc.
Text © 2024 Jane Wilsher. Illustrations © 2024 Teo Georgiev

First published in 2024 by Ivy Kids, an imprint of The Quarto Group.
100 Cummings Center, Suite 265D, Beverly, MA 01915, USA.
T +1 978-282-9590 www.Quarto.com

The right of Jane Wilsher to be indentified as the author and Teo Georgiev
to be identified as the illustrator of this work has been asserted by them in accordance
with the Copyright, Designs and Patents Act, 1988 (United Kingdom).

A CIP record for this book is available from the Library of Congress.

ISBN 978-0-7112-9264-2
eISBN -978-0-7112-9266-6

The illustrations were created digitally.
Set in Busy Day, Filson Soft, and Blackberry Macarons Sans

Published by Georgia Buckthorn • Edited by Alex Hithersay
Designed by Kathryn Davies and Sasha Moxon • Art directed by Karissa Santos
Production by Dawn Cameron

Manufactured in Villatuerta, Spain GC062024

9 8 7 6 5 4 3 2 1

RECYCLED
Paper made from
recycled material
FSC
www.fsc.org
FSC® C007507

Print product with financial
climate contribution
ClimatePartner.com/15610-2404-1001

This book reports information which may be of general interest to the reader. The activities set out within this book shall take place under close adult supervision. Adults should handle or assist with any potentially harmful tools or materials. Furthermore, there is the possibility of allergic or other adverse reactions from the use of any product mentioned in this book. The reader should fully inform themselves and should consult with a medical practitioner before they attempt or allow any child to attempt any activity set out within this book. The publisher and the author make no representations or warranties with respect to the accuracy, completeness or currency of the contents of this book, and specifically disclaim, without limitation, any implied warranties of merchantability or fitness for a particular purpose and exclude all liability to the extent permitted by law for any injury, illness, damage, liability, or loss incurred, directly or indirectly, from the use or application of any of the contents of this book. If you need medical, physical, or mental help please consult a doctor, readings do not substitute for medical advice or treatment.